"Stir Up The Gift"

T's Coloring Book

Terry Holt

10

Terry Holt

P.O. Box 38285
Spanish Lake, MO 63138

http://cafepress.com/MOREPublishers

www.ArtistRising.com

http:/createspace.com

Layout by M.O.R.E. Publishers

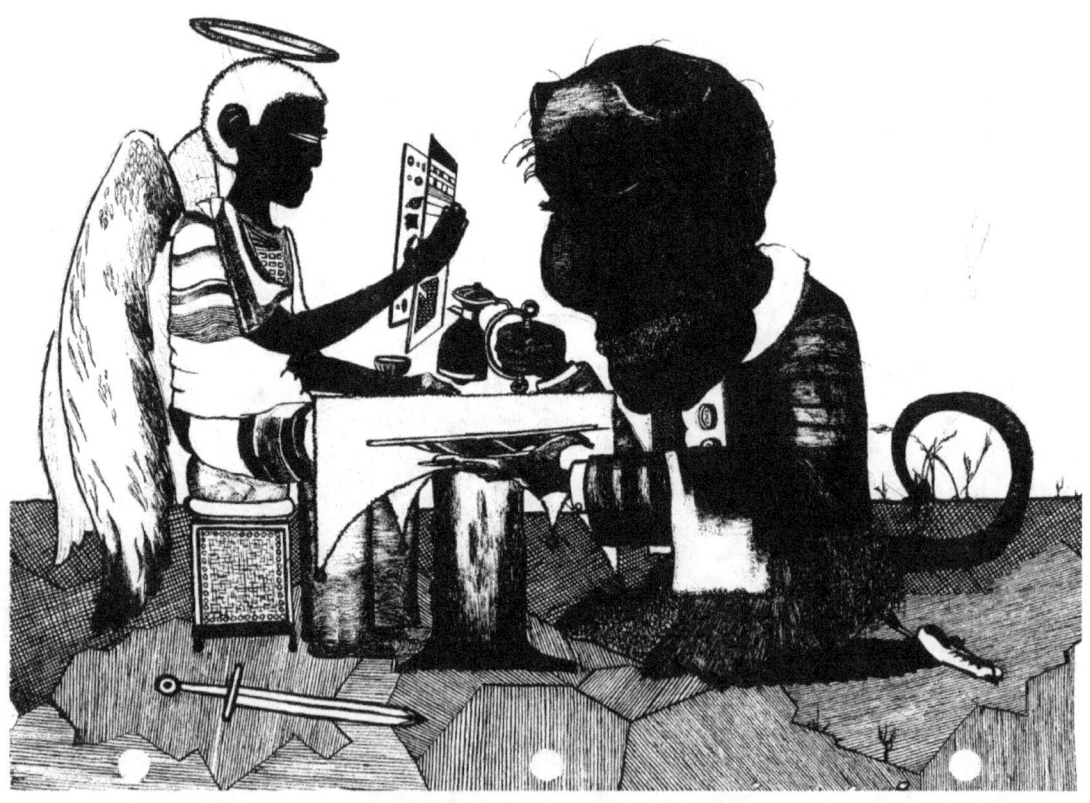

The Angel and the Devil"

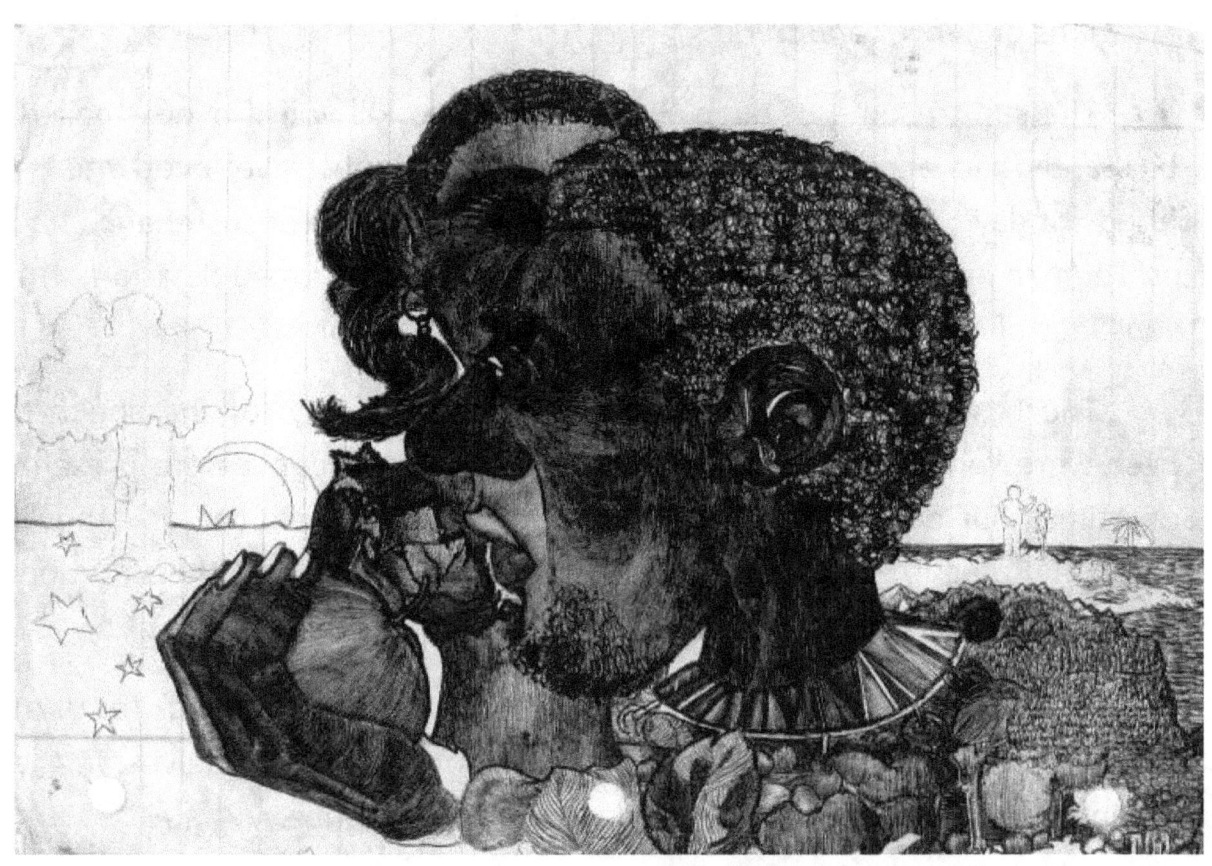

"UnNatural Hood"

Unnatural Hood! (Chapter 1)

By Terry Holt

From the sky, the area that was once our neighborhood had now resembled what could be compared to a junkyard! Fires were across every other block. Some of them were at the conjunctions of the four-way stop signs, while others stood in shambles of old smothering heaps. They now were unoccupied semi-structures that held the material of our days of old and youth. There wasn't very much food available, so daily....almost 60% of time was spent scheming on how to successfully curve the ever- present sensations of hunger and thirst.

The sun to some of us in then-o-day could kill you if over-exposed. You barely had enough moisture to sweat, let alone travel over intense periods of day. So many years of neglecting the tactics of sustenance had cost humanity gravely millions of hours in front of the television, the thousands of days before the video games and what-not.

The basements here and there provided the best of the shelters. These were kept intensely clean because the sick and dying were present. Sometimes our dear friends would get well enough, while others - they'd fade away to death. They probably weren't too upset about the situation. There was nothing to do at day nor was there anymore whilst night.

There were no guarantees that the angels would come back for us at all. Who could deal with us? We started to think within ourselves. In the present state of mind.....we were all next to non existence.

www.MOREPublishers.biz

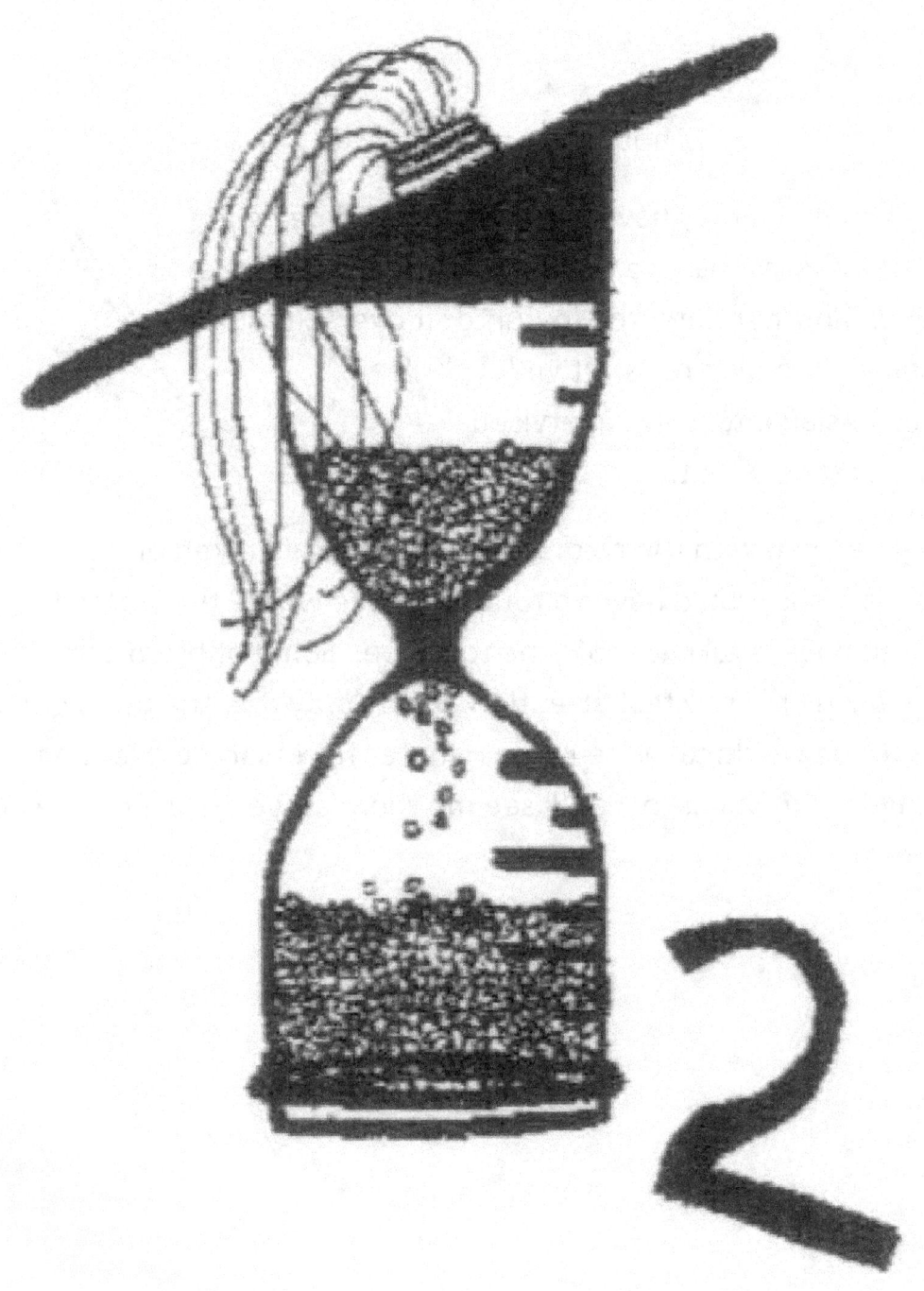

From the book **Twelve Again**

About the Artist

The art that you may have seen comes from being in constant atmospheres that are either too dangerous to relax properly, or on another note, too joyful to sit over extended periods of time. The pictures start with light lead. Afterward comes an intensely supervised microscopic ink stretch-out.

Since I've been with the colors, my pictures have taken on new dimensions, as if you would have to touch it to see where the surface started. These images take lots of time to shape. Some of them completely absorb me – taking my strictest attention. I only pray that the people that may have interest would take the many minutes necessary to examine every centimeter. In doing so, you'll see me there as well – just my way of waving hello!

Terry Holt

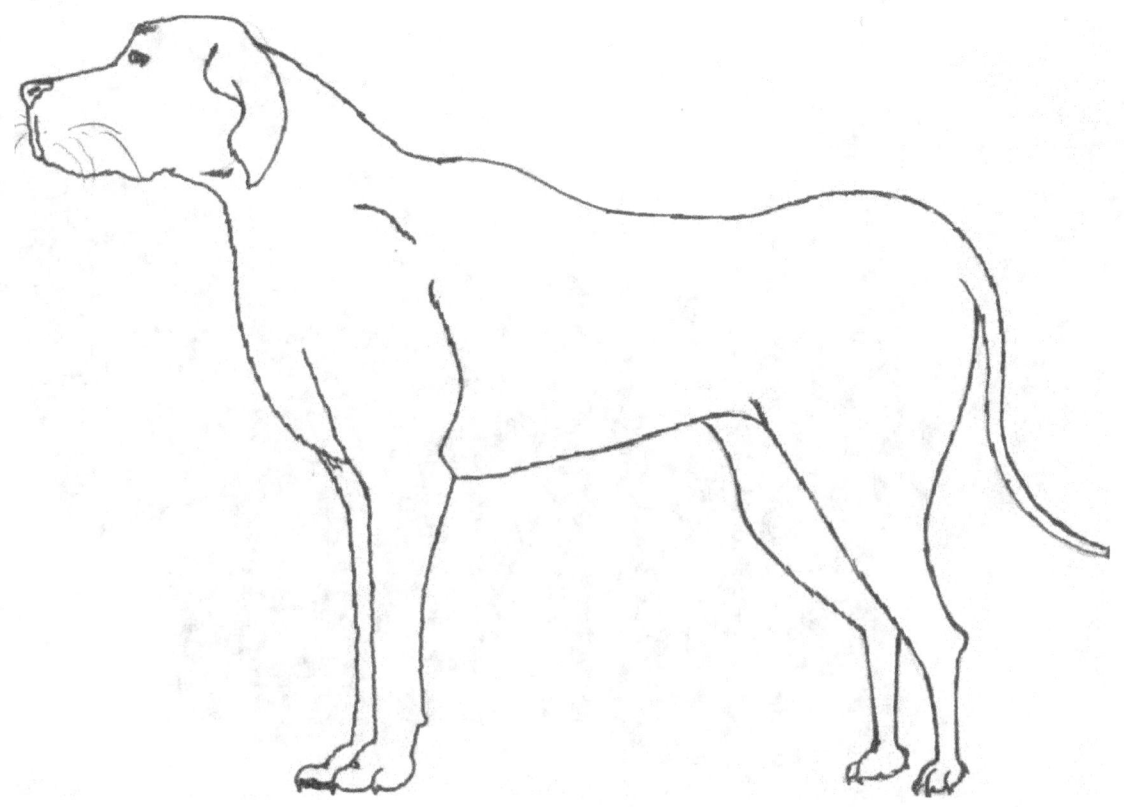

"I'm straight"

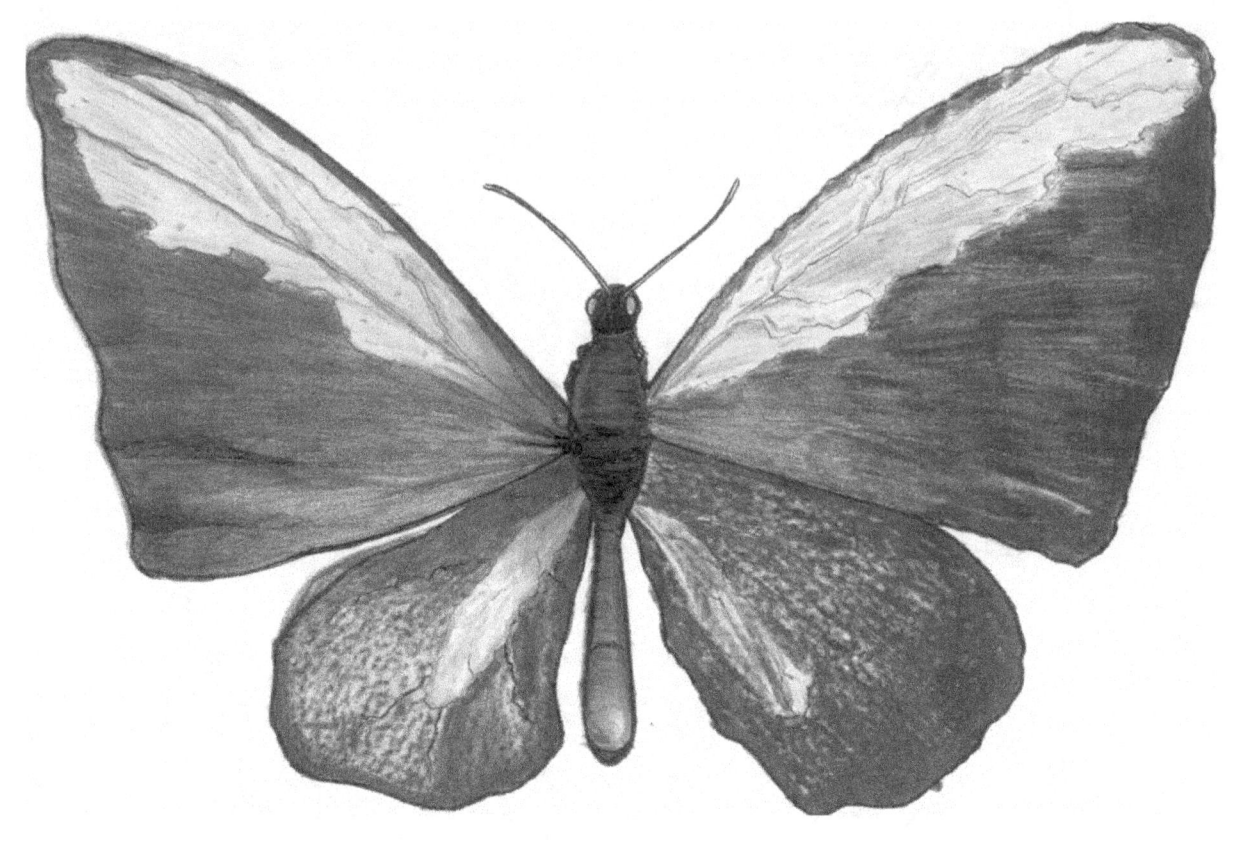

"The Butterfly"

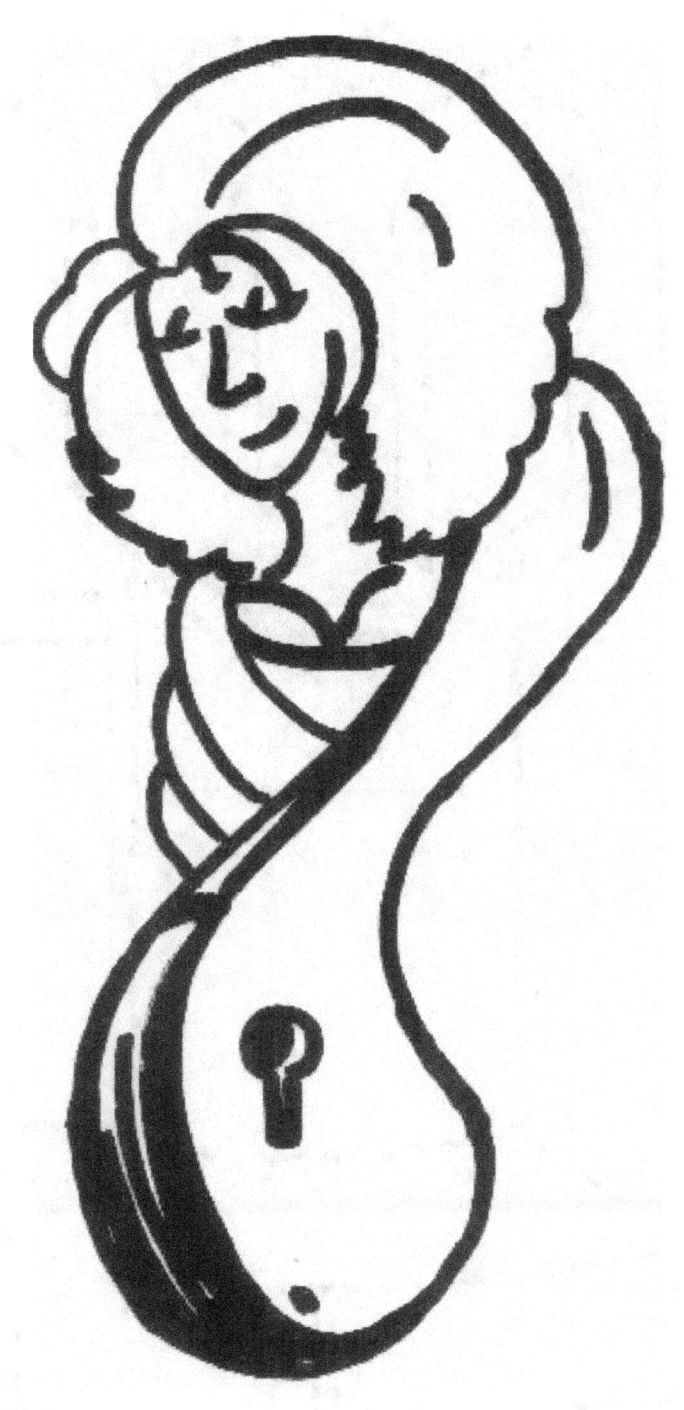

"Lady"

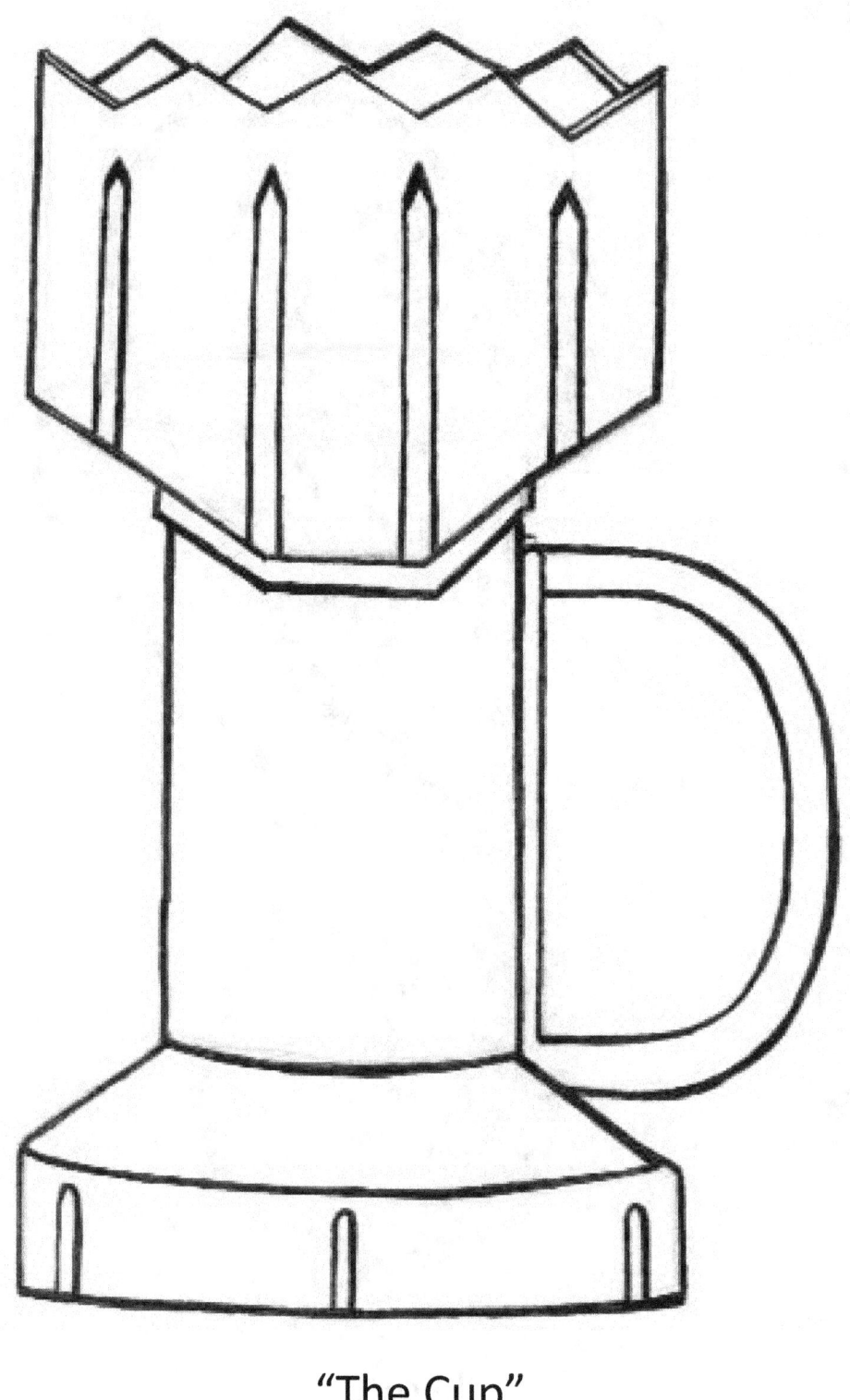

"The Cup"

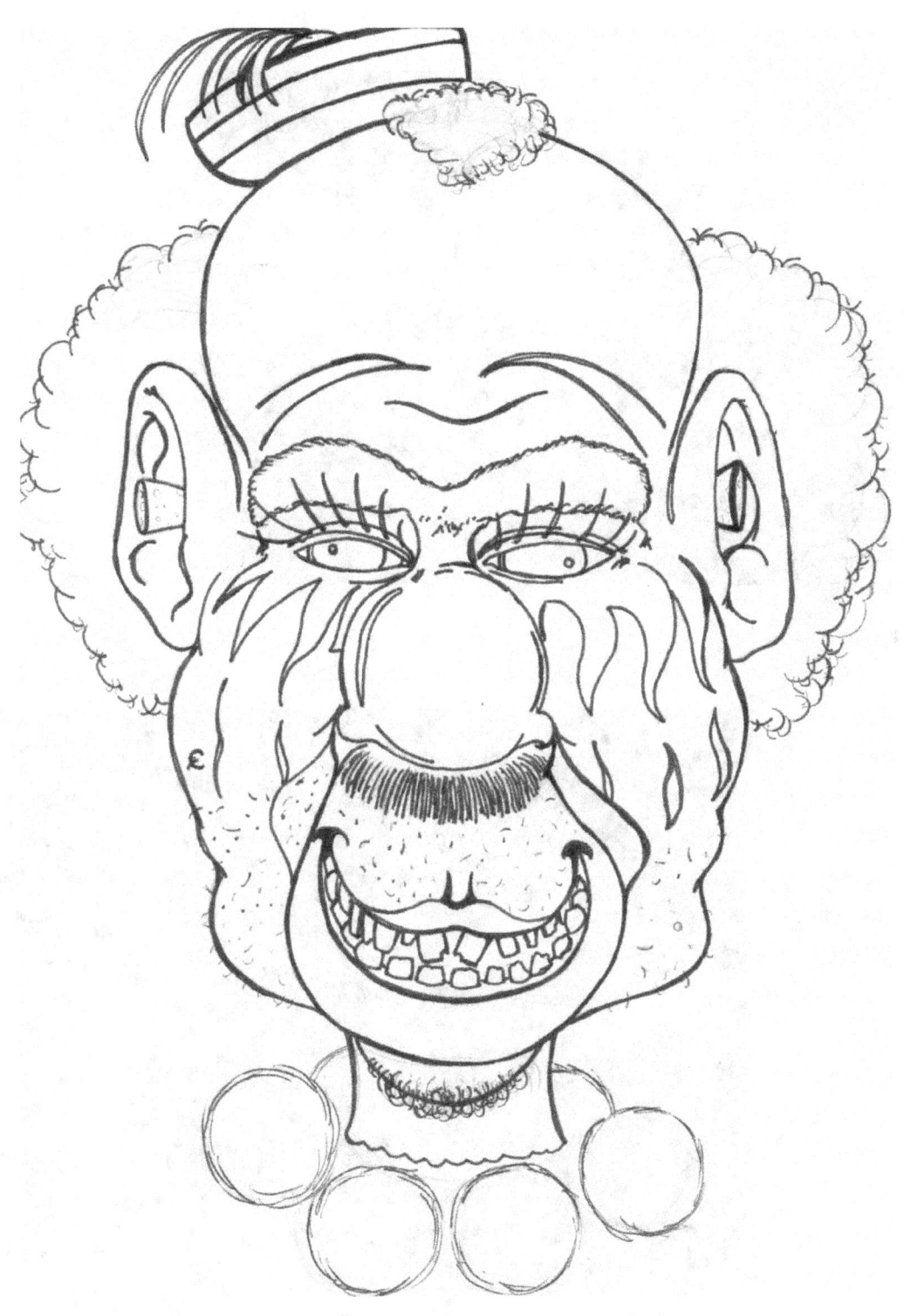

"Clown"

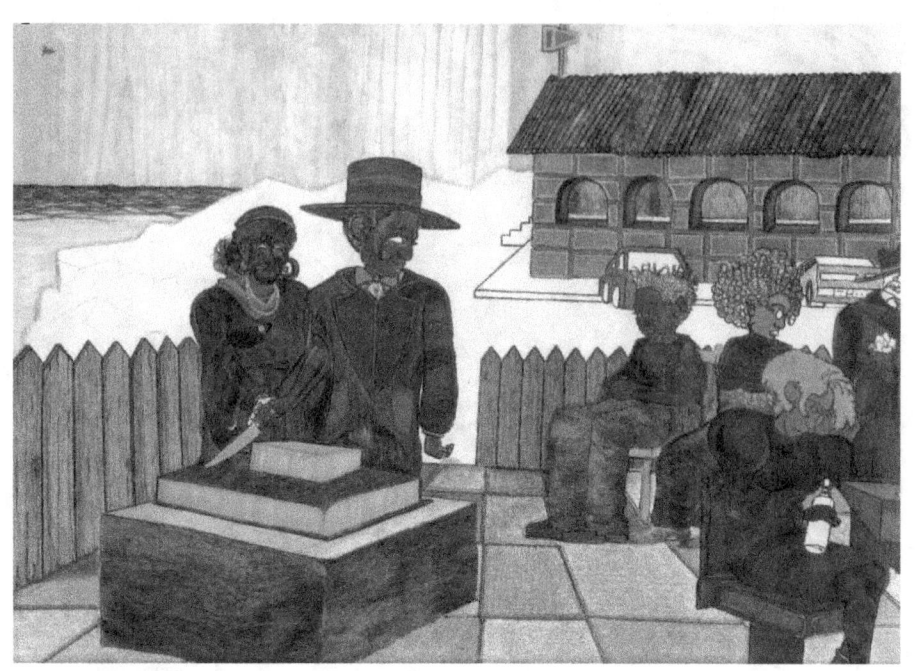

"Cold Slice"

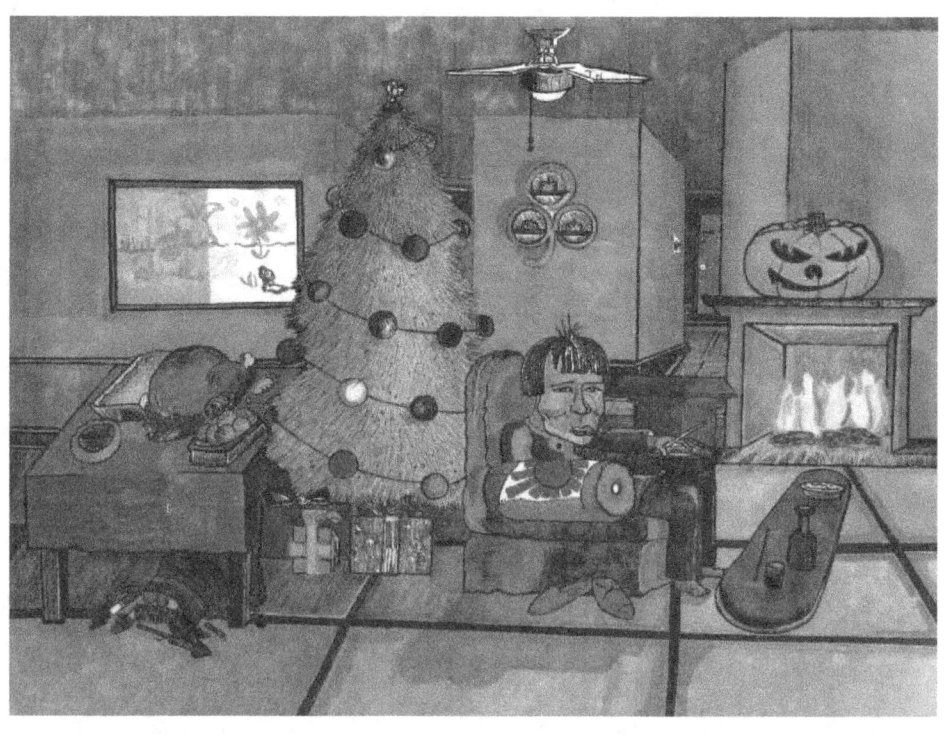

"7th Holiday"

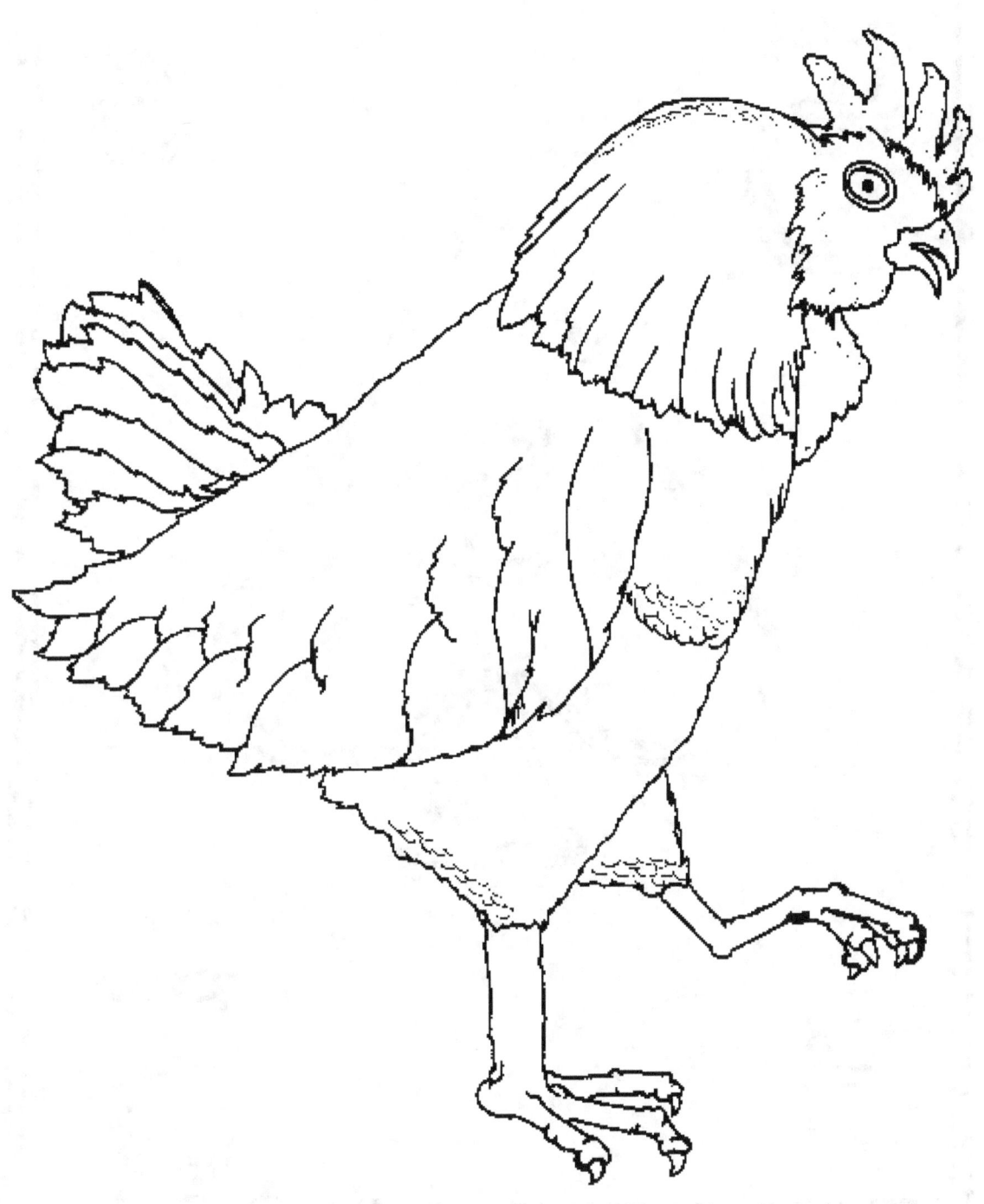

"Country Rooster"

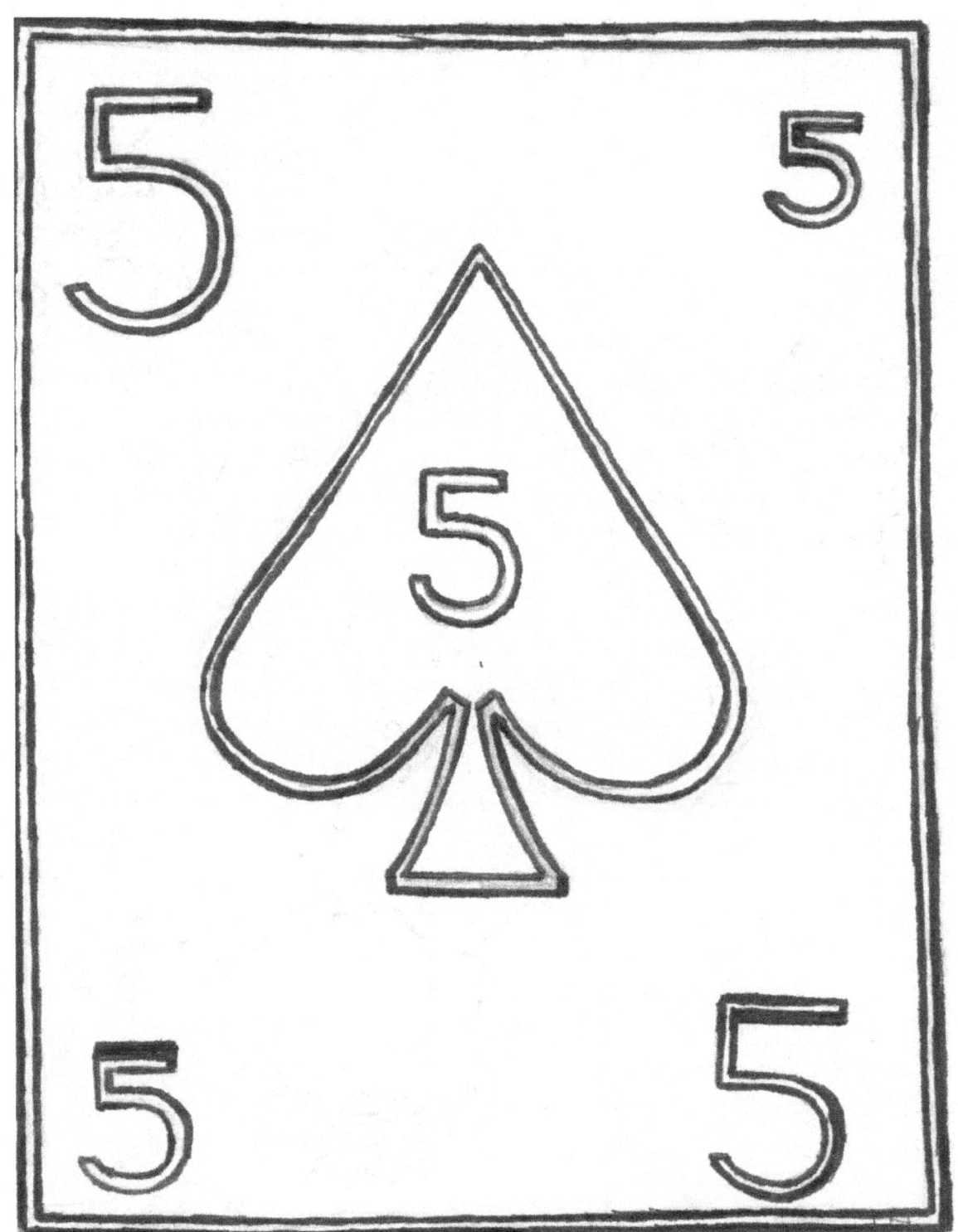

"Spade"

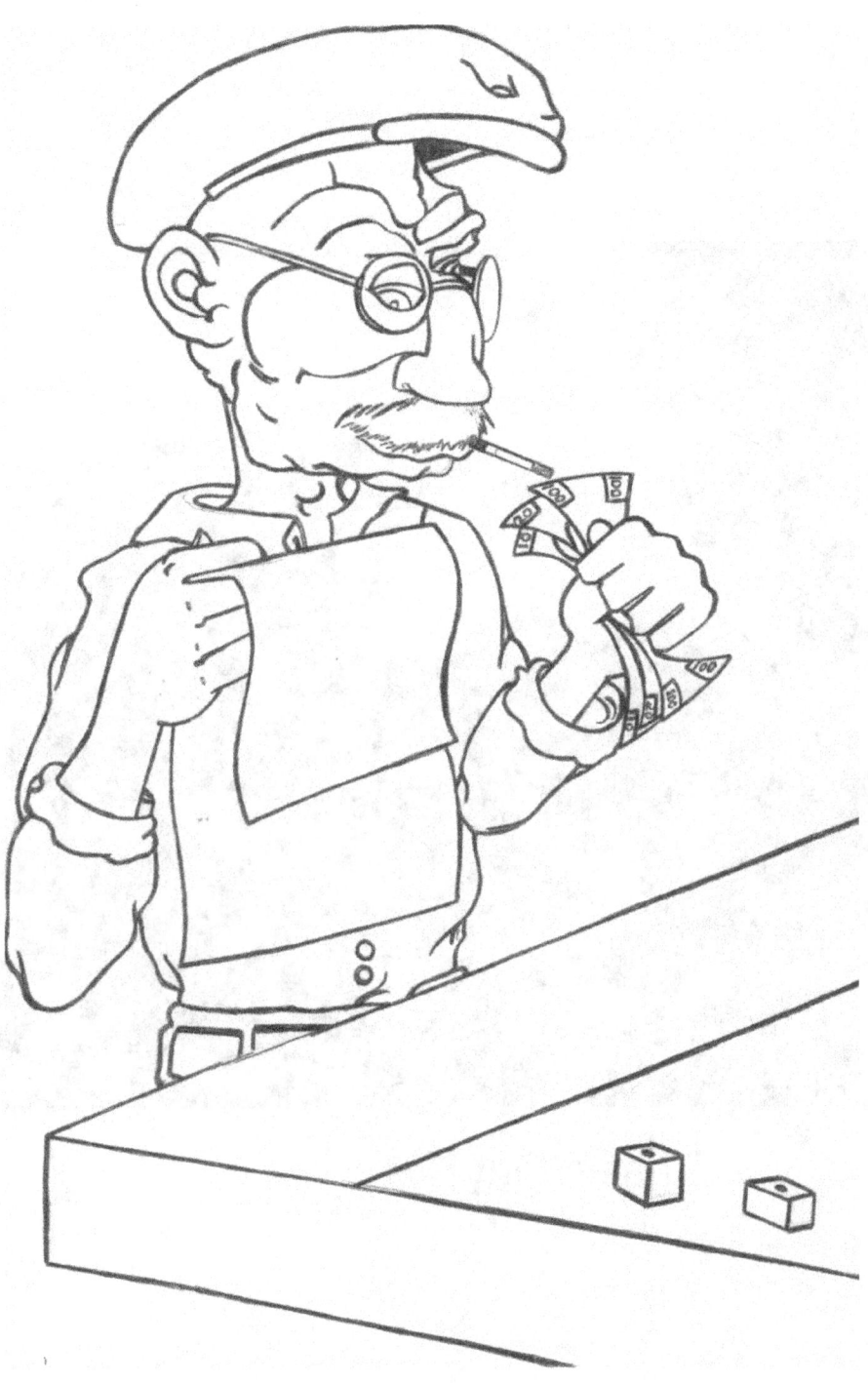

"The Gambler"

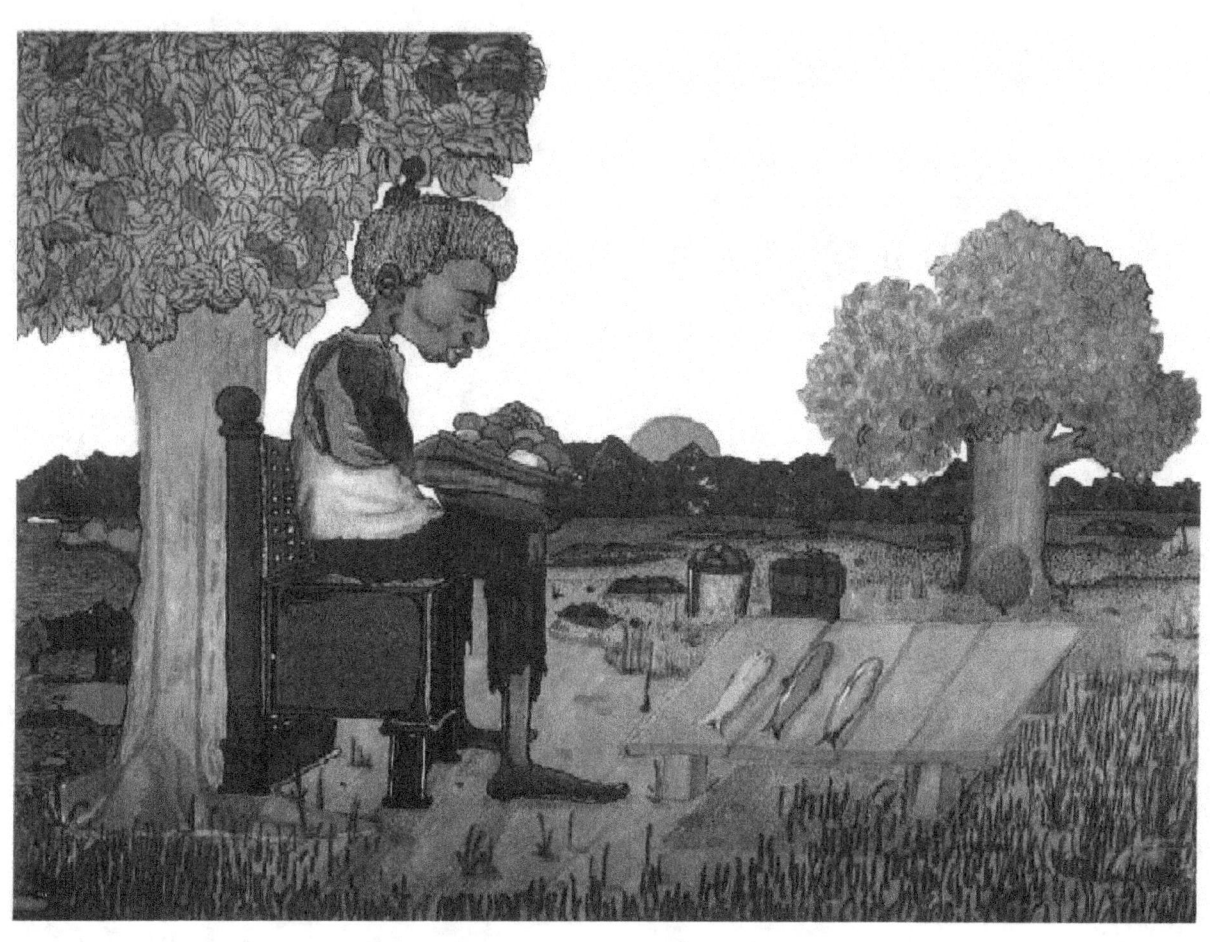

"What A Day!"

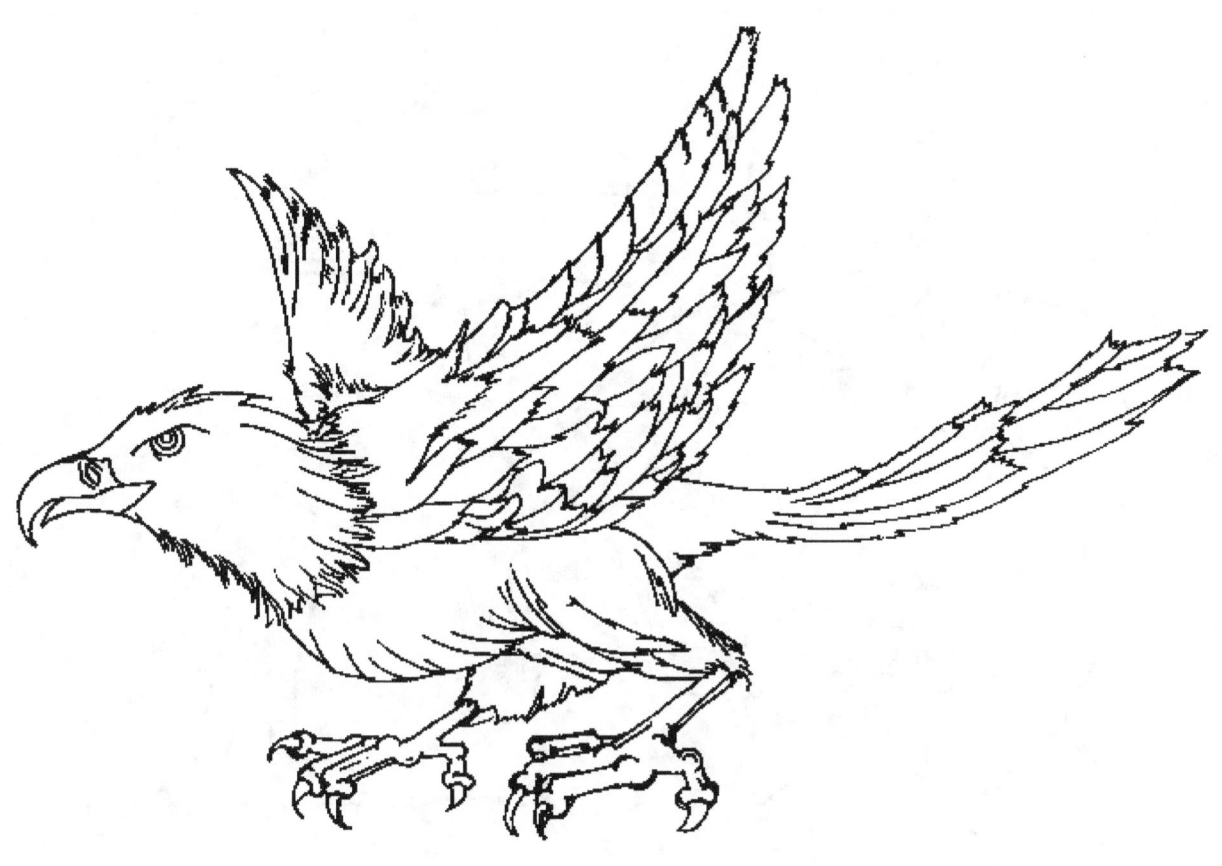

"An Eagle"

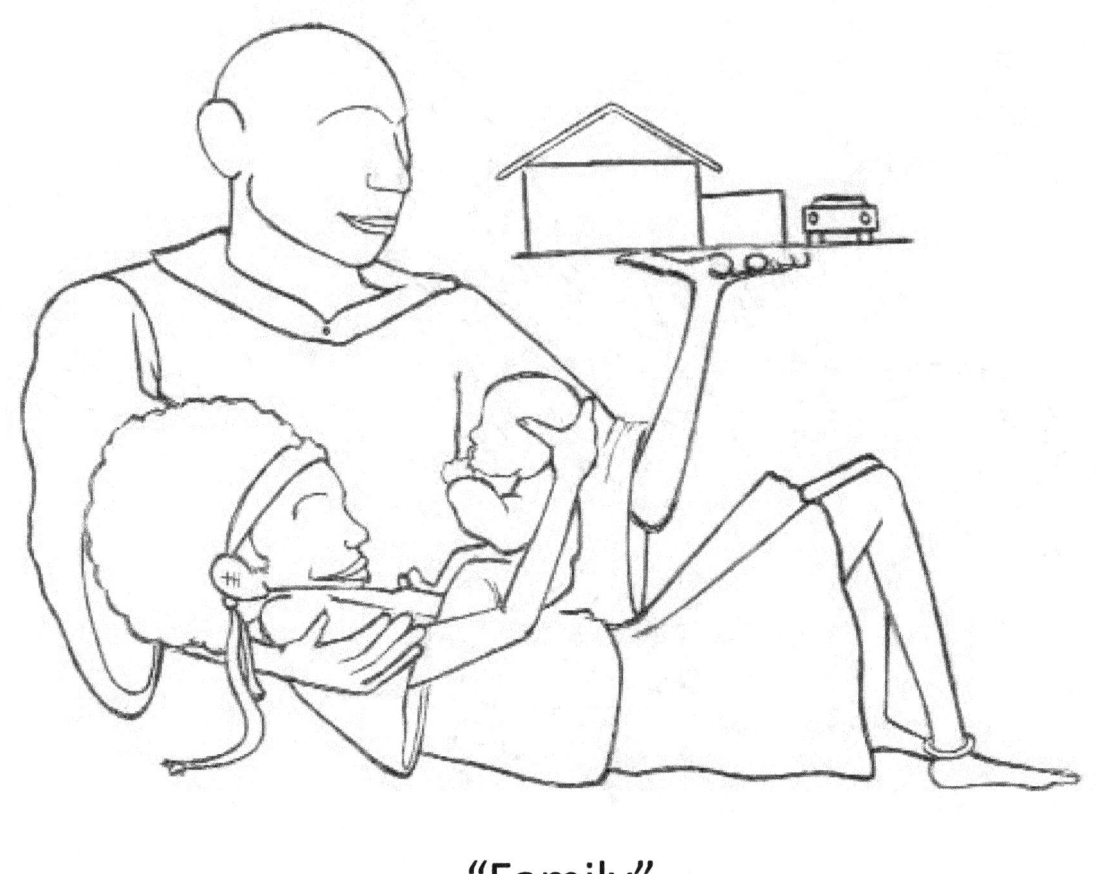

"Family"

From <u>Poems and Praise</u> by Gertrude R. Anderson

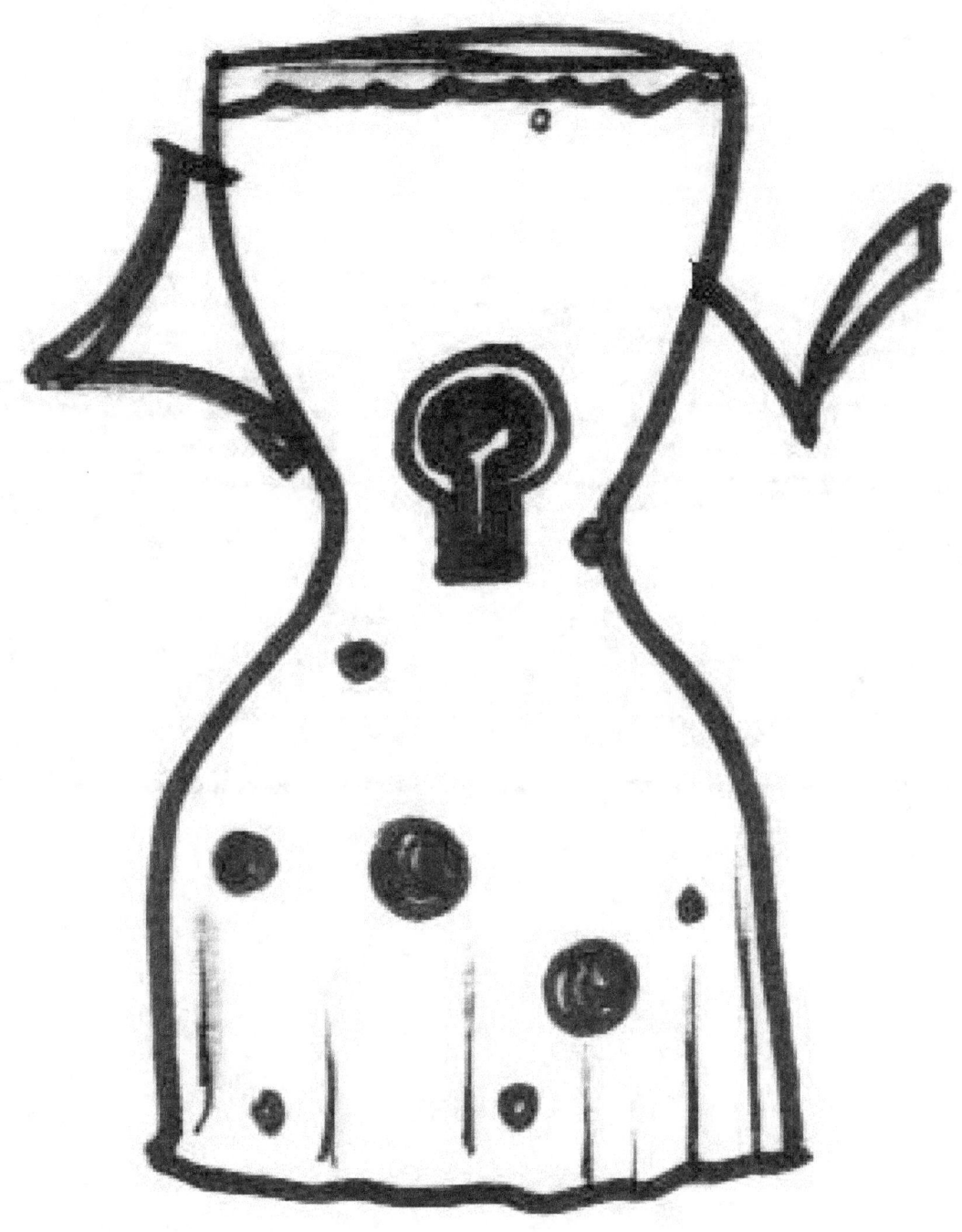

"Liquid Virgin"

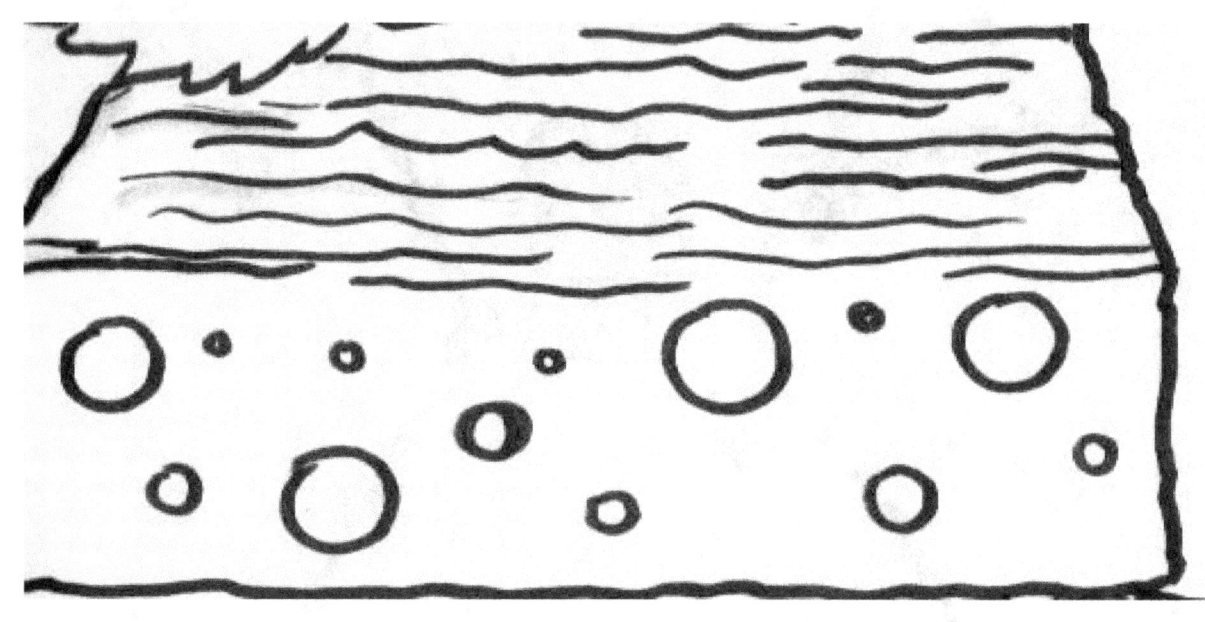

"The Bath"

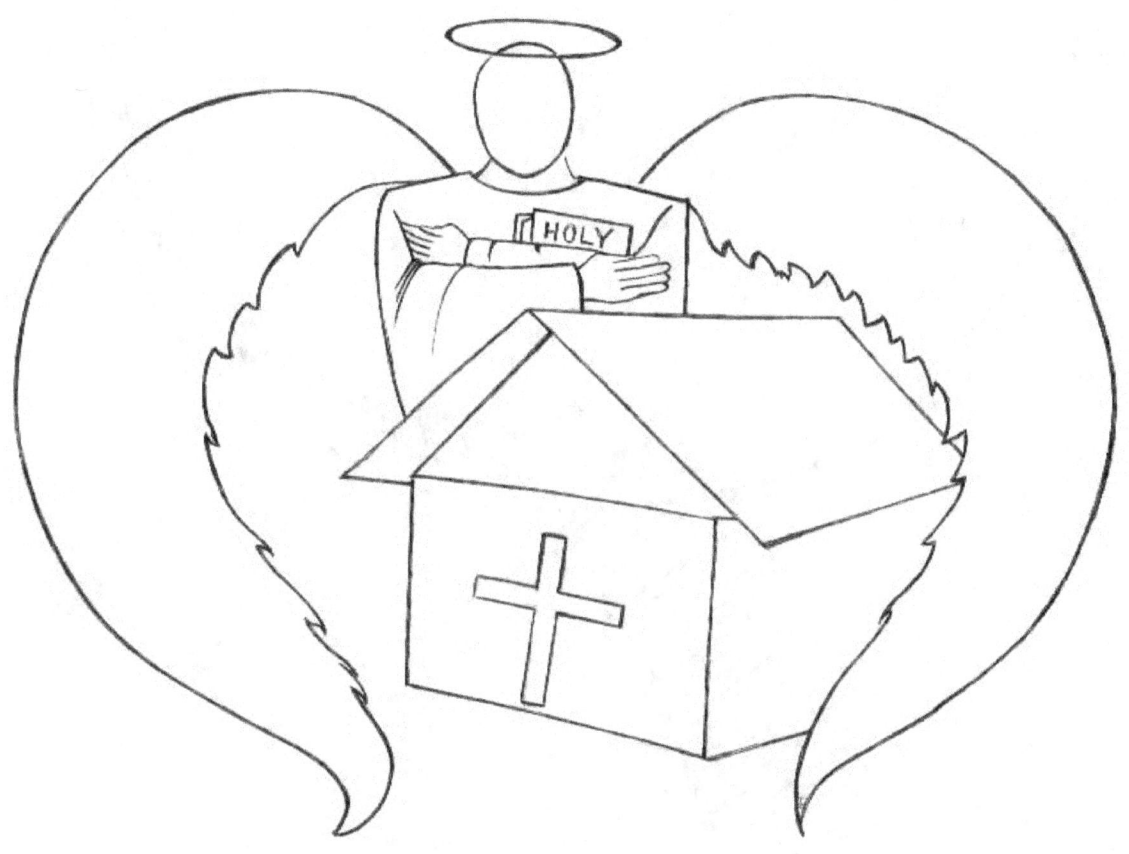

"Love"

From <u>Poems and Praise</u> by Gertrude R. Anderson

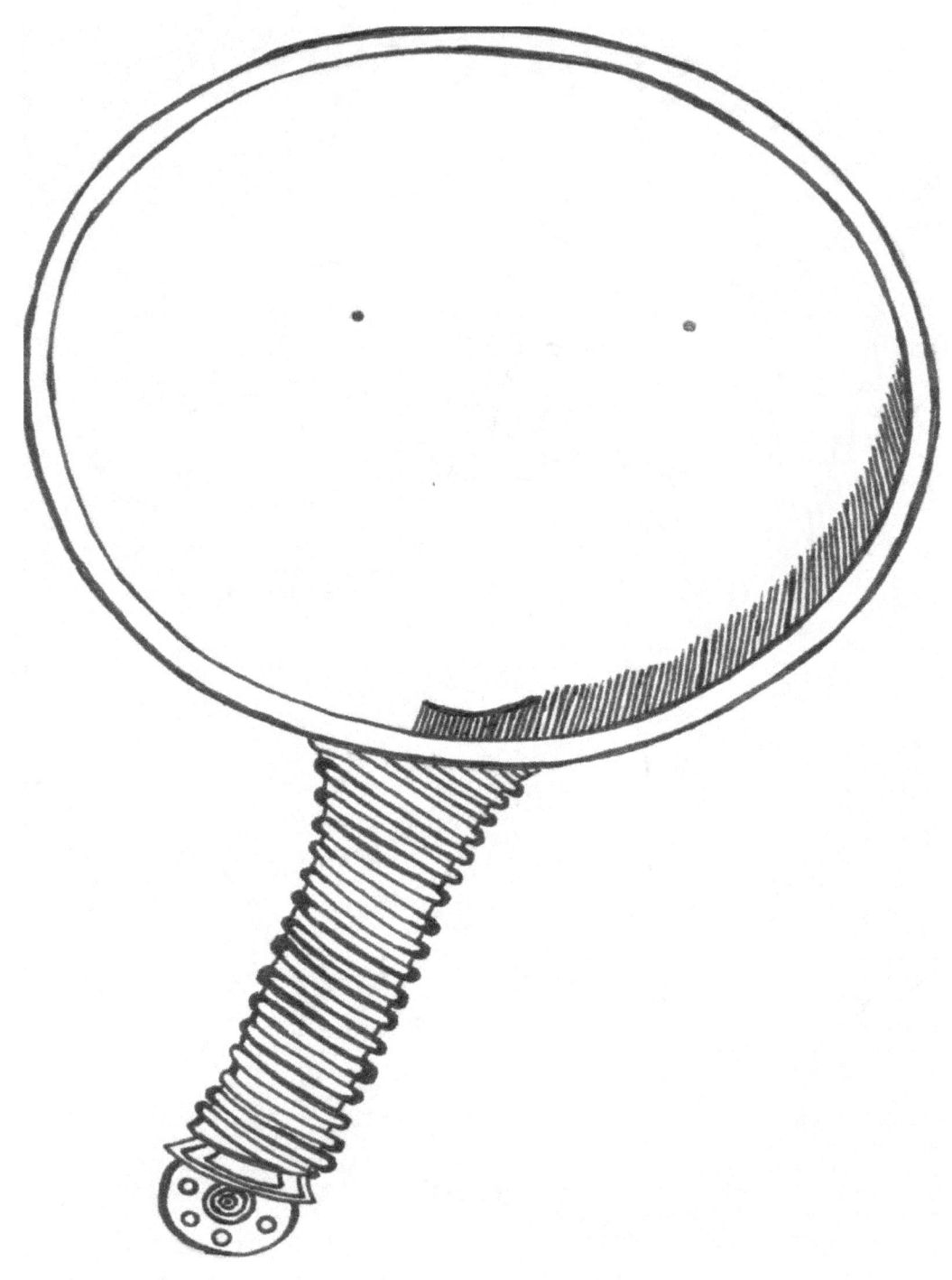

"The Mirror"

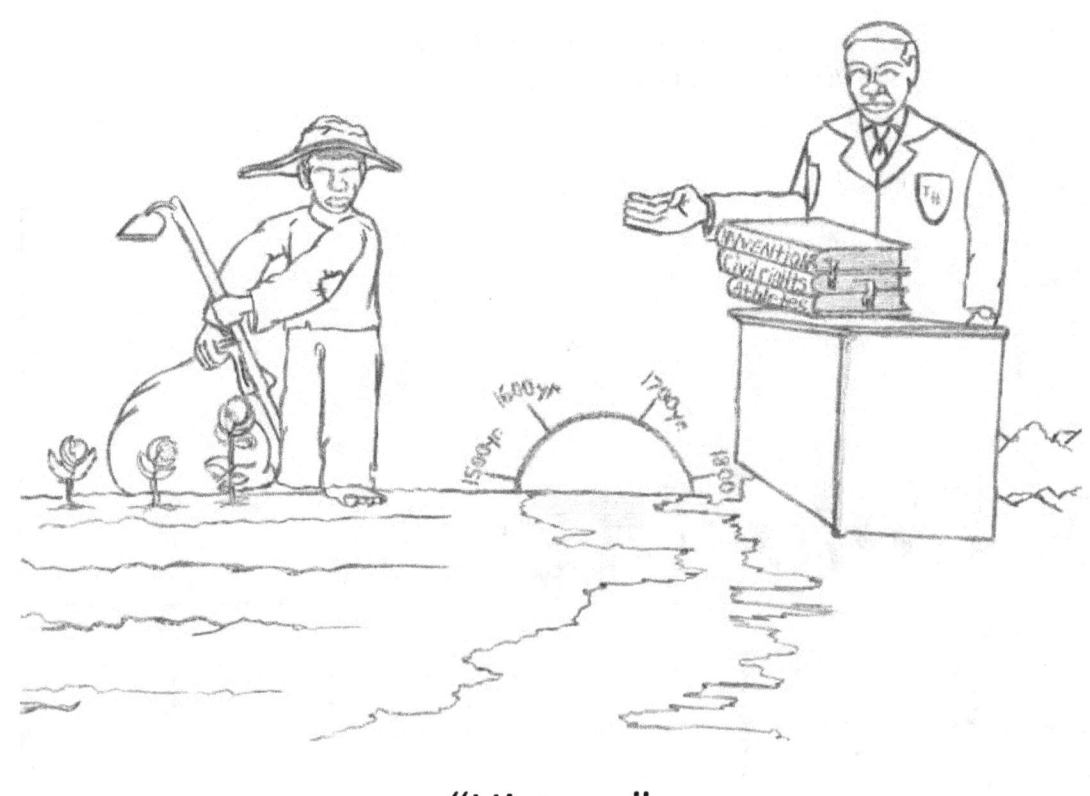

"History"

From <u>Poems and Praise</u> by Gertrude R. Anderson

Credits:

Editing and publicity -   Angelee C. Grider

Layout   -   M.O.R.E. Publishers
                        Edwin M.T. Grider, Editor

"Stir Up The Gift"

T's Coloring
Book

Terry Holt

10

www.ingramcontent.com/pod-product-compliance
Lightning Source LLC
Chambersburg PA
CBHW081250170526
45165CB00009B/3271